THE CHRISTIAN

IN

THE MATERIAL WORLD

THE CHRISTIAN

IN

THE MATERIAL WORLD

by

Giovanni Battista Cardinal Montini

HELICON PRESS

Baltimore

from the original Italian *Il Cristiano e il Benessere Temporale*
edited by Ufficio Studi Arcivescovili di Milano

translated by Reverend Michael M. McManus,
Secretary, Apostolic Delegation, Canada

with the permission of the Ordinary of Montreal,
December 29, 1963, No. 741.

HELICON, 1964

First Edition, December 1963
Second Edition, January 1964

Library of Congress Catalog Card Number 64-14666

Helicon Press, Inc.
1120 N. Calvert Street
Baltimore, Maryland 21202

TABLE OF CONTENTS

The problem of the material world springs from the fact that we are immersed in the things of this world. Economic prosperity absorbs us more and more, as though it wanted first to attract us, then to enchant us and finally to enchain us.

INTRODUCTION

Among the numerous problems that arise from our effort to direct our spirit towards the Lord, one in particular merits reflection. It derives from the fact that we are immersed in the things of this world, things which absorb our time, our energies and our interests. We realise at once that this is in some way an obstacle to our union with Christ. Our concern with temporal things renders difficult a spiritual involvement with Christ, and often impedes it. Secular interests limit religious interests. Our Lord told us we cannot serve two masters, the kingdom of this world and the kingdom of God.

Today this problem is becoming ever more acute, as we witness a steady rise in our standard of living. This absorbs an ever-increasing share of our attention and lessens our capacity for a supernatural religious life. This is true not only of actions such as recollection, prayer, the frequenting of the sacraments, the religious celebration of feast days. It also affects our attitude, that is to say, the attention paid to spiritual values and to the decisive importance of our relationship with God.[1]

We wish therefore to pause for a while to consider this aspect of our common experience, the obstacle placed in the way of an adequate contact with religious reality by the things of this world. This is a thought familiar enough to all of us, since it is the basis for much of Christian education, preaching, ascetic and spiritual practices. It is a matter which acquires a greater urgency at this time of increased economic progress.

---

1 This important book was written by the present Pope during his last months as Cardinal Archbishop of Milan. He urged at that time, in connection with the impending feast of Easter 1963, that as: "we are setting out on our journey towards Easter, towards that meeting with Christ which must bring to our lives happiness and a sense of awareness of participating in the drama of His and our Redemption, we must prepare ourselves" for "this regenerating event."

This preparation demands of us that we turn towards Christ, "that we redirect ourselves towards Him."

One must walk through the world with a religious sense of the divine presence, rather of a divine expectation which is on the one hand deeply hidden and on the other openly manifest.

. . . . . And God saw that His work was good and He blessed it . . . . . (Gen. 1: 4)

From evangelical poverty flows liberty of the spirit. Freed of the fascination for an inferior good and for material things, we learn to act and love spiritually.

PART ONE

PART ONE

Welfare Society and Christianity

Is this economic progress real? Those who are competent to pronounce judgment say it is. Moreover, almost all of us have had some experience of it. The present prosperity is not everywhere the same nor is it yet sufficient for everybody, but one has the impression that we are approaching a point in which economic needs will be better satisfied.

We do not wish to dwell too long on the manifold consequences of this characteristic phenomenon of our time. Hunger, misery, unemployment, private insecurity, though they are in themselves very important, must someday disappear from our midst. The great social problems of the last century which continue to disturb the world may well be solved or at least diminished. Social classes must draw closer together. The standard of living for all ought to be more uniform. The excessive strain of gaining a livelihood should cease. Avarice, which amasses the goods of this world only to hoard them for itself, must diminish. The dependence of some men upon others, which results from a lack of the necessities of life, ought to decrease.

Changes in relationships within the family, in popular culture, in the mobility of populations — such things have already changed the face of society and altered the course of history. They are beginning to change the life of the individual. Let us take a careful look at this transformation of the world's scene.

Two feelings fill the soul in the face of this social wonder. The first is admiration for those who are working for economic progress, for the scientists, the technicians and planners on the one hand, for skilled and unskilled workers on the other — management and labor, the brain and the hand.

This admiration also includes capital, understood as the generating, directing and instrumental part of the economic transformation of our society, and work, understood as the human, executive and organizing factor which, with sweat and suffering, has made such a transformation possible.

The improvement in relations between these two co-efficients of modern civilization gives birth to another feeling, which is one of serene hope. Indeed, we ask ourselves if these two must still be conceived as opposing forces locked in a perennial and fatal struggle inherent in the very fact of their encounter. Today it is possible, and even necessary, to regard them as two elements which complement each other organically, productively and socially. They are parallel terms — capital and work, economic means and human effort, direction and execution — or dual terms expressing a mutual interest which seems to spring from the nature of the duality itself. This mutual interest should coordinate and never oppose the two forces which make up one reality. Their relationship one with the other should be marked not with opposition or guarded respect but with collaboration and solidarity.

We now wish to consider more closely the effect so great a phenomenon has on the religious and moral life. First, let us consider its negative aspects.

The first of these is a practical materialism. The age of economic progress emphasises, above all, the general anxiety to reach a better standard of living. This is not anything bad. On the contrary, it can be a good in itself, if this search for prosperity does not paralyze the progress of the human spirit. That work be a law for all, that it be part of the dignity of man and of nations, that it reveal itself as the principal source of the material well-being of all,

This objection demands reflection on the part of the Christian, because there is growing up around him an attitude of diffidence, of estrangement and also of hostility.

It is an objection which is taking root in circles noteworthy for their trust in the primacy of the economic factor: the world of Capitalism and Marxism. It flourishes also in the world of youth lacking a true perspective of life. Unhappily, we see signs of its growth every day, so much so that we think it is one of the most serious and urgent questions of our time. That question is to verify the relationship which ought to exist between Christian life and modern life, the former understood as faith in the Gospel message and the latter understood as life pervaded by the penetration and mastery of the temporal order. Hence we are concerned with examining the meaning the material world should have for the Christian.

The Christian Vision of the Material World

We will simplify our enquiry by reducing it to a three-fold observation. First of all, we must recognize the fact that the Christian is *a priori* an optimist in his view of worldly goods. He is not hostile towards them, he favours them; he is not disturbed by but attracted to them; he is not fearful but sympathetic towards them. If he handles them prudently it is because he respects them, and knows instinctively that there are other values higher still.

We find confirmation for such an attitude of mind every time our ministry causes us to visit one or another of the great projects of our day — the new factories, modern buildings and large commercial centers. Precisely because of our religious principles, we know immediately that we cannot ignore achievements of this sort, much less condemn them.

Instead, there come to mind the marvellous and mysterious words, again and again repeated in the Bible, which tell of a similar admiration which God felt for the works of his creation: "And God saw that it was good." The maker of the universe was satisfied with his work. God saw his own image reflected in his creatures. He admired their order, movement, grandeur, beauty and depth. He heard the hymn rising from the cosmos he created. He measured the strength of his own power and freedom.

This would be a stupendous subject for meditation: to look at the essence of things through the eyes of God. We would immediately be dazzled. Perhaps this could be the resurgence of a renewal of religion for the man of tomorrow which the scientific world of yesterday lost.

But for the moment — by way of an analogy which, however slight, is both edifying and authorized by St. Paul when he commanded us to be imitators of God — we wish only to assume a similar attitude toward the works of men. And are not these also works of intelligence, of patience and toil, of usefulness and beauty? For this they merit our applause, and for two other reasons they recommend themselves to our religious piety. First of all because, within our earthly horizon, the work of man develops the works of God. It uncovers their deep potential, brings them to light, unveils their wonders, deploys their energies and enhances their benefits.

Secondly, since it is in the nature of modern work to try to reduce the worker's fatigue as well as to satisfy the needs of society, the consequent benefits are both economic and social. Thus, it is the work of human intelligence and charity which we admire in the best of modern achievements. And it is for this that they merit our appreciation and gratitude.

The energy with which modern man seeks to understand, dominate and utilize nature, putting it at his service, must be considered a worthy response to the endowment given man by God. The voice of God reveals to us the sense of the world: "Fill the earth and make it yours." The nature which surrounds us is a wonderful invitation to explore, conquer and possess.

This invitation is not intended to limit man to the realms of this world. It moves him to begin a journey or even to place his foot upon a ladder which will lead him back to his origin, back to God. Work and the conquest of the physical world are nothing but a journey which must lead man to the original source. One must walk through this world with a religious sense of the divine presence, rather of a divine expectation which is on the one hand deeply hidden and on the other openly manifest.

This journey holds a surprise in store for us: an encounter with the Word of God come into the world as man: an encounter with the Incarnation. Our experience of the created world is transformed into an extraordinary adventure, into a magnificent revelation. Here is what St. Paul says:

"Everything is for you . . . and you for Christ and Christ for God."

And he adds:

"All that rings true, all that commands reverence and all that makes for right: all that is pure, all that is lovely, all that is gracious in the telling . . . let this be the argument of your thoughts."

The Christian is not insensitive to the world of nature or to the material realm. He is no escapist nor is he lost in abstractions. Neither is he absorbed in the angelism of the spiritual world. Quite the contrary, he is one who can have the highest and most complete view of temporal values, who can approach them with the greatest realism, who can best deal with them. For example, we consider honesty an essential virtue in the Christian profession — is it not also a basic requirement for the proper use of economic goods?

Christianity is not an obstacle to modern progress because it does not consider modern progress only in its technical and economic aspects but in its total development. Temporal goods can certainly help the full development of man, but they do not constitute the ideal of human perfection nor the essence of social progress.

The Christian sees in temporal goods the work and the gifts of God. As such he admires them and puts them to his use, but they do not become his idol. He always remembers the first commandment: "Thou shalt have no other God but me." It is there that the drama of the confrontation between the Christian and the temporal order is born.

The Spirit of Poverty

Here we make the second observation, whose negative import seems to contradict the optimism of the first. It is this: the Christian is warned in his catechism that in the things of this world, especially in the organization human (or diabolical) malice has given them, there can be and often is a profound and inexplicable disorder. Neither human nature nor men's actions are always good. Evil exists around us even without our willing it. If it were not so, the struggles for human progress which are recorded in history would have no meaning.

The Christian is equally alive to this aspect of reality. He is not naive, nor is he passive or blissfully optimistic. He senses intuitively the tragic in life, and is attuned to the groaning of creation as it awaits a regeneration.

Thanks to the wizardry of modern man, the forces of nature can also unleash formidable threats and dire ruin. The atomic bomb is teaching us this. Whoever is wise, whoever is Christian, cannot but be alarmed by these grave perils, inherent in progress itself, once it is withdrawn from the primacy of moral law.

It is precisely because of these higher moral laws that the Christian is prudent and watchful when dealing with the goods of this world. They can constitute a strong temptation toward the subversion of the moral order. They do this not only by the immense destructive power which they possess, but even more by the way in which they tend to insinuate this fatal illusion: that the goods of this earth are the final and supreme purpose of human activity, that in themselves they can constitute paradise, in themselves give happiness. Temporal goods, which were meant to mirror the divine, become instead instruments of delusion and of enslavement. Where once they were paths by which man might go to God, they now lead him away.

This is why the Christian listens to the words of Christ, who made poverty the first beatitude of the kingdom of heaven, words for him still true and sovereign. Poverty is a defence which offers man immunity against the possible deception of the things of this world.

Today, however, it seems absurd to eulogize poverty. Riches have taken on such an importance that praise, or even simple tolerance of poverty, seems ridiculous.

We must explain this poverty, upon which the religious spirit of Christianity is based. Is it a question of economic poverty? Yes, it is that, but with two qualifications.

Our Lord did not impose misery upon us, the privation of things necessary for life. He taught us to ask our Father in heaven for the bread we need: He himself multiplied it to feed the crowd that had followed him. He himself recommended alms-giving, which is a remedy for indigence, and he recognized labor for wages and profit as the law of temporal life. He was himself the "son of a carpenter."

Secondly, economic poverty is represented in the Gospels not as a good in itself but as a reflection of another kind of poverty, one indispensable for a Christian: poverty of spirit.

To understand poverty of spirit we must turn to the saints and doctors of the Church, who have spoken of it so often. Here we limit ourselves to recalling the phrase of St. Ambrose, who understands poverty of spirit as humility of spirit.

The Gospel, in effect, speaks of a state of soul, of an ascetic poverty, without establishing a necessary relationship with the economic condition of the Christian. Even a man in extreme poverty, if he puts his highest aspirations and his complete confidence in economic goods, could be lacking in Christian poverty. And conversely, a rich man who refused to make economic goods his ambition, his joy, and the measure of his life, could possess Christian poverty. This is why one can understand that we must speak to all of that poverty which is lodged in the heart, irrespective of economic and social conditions, even though these may be markedly affected by this interior virtue.

The Meaning and Value of
Evangelical Poverty

Evangelical poverty is a warning of man's insufficiency and his consequent need for God. It is a denial of the primacy of the economic and of the capacity of temporal goods to satisfy the heart of man. It is a renunciation of the search to fulfil our destiny in this world, or to find safeguards against what are deep and fatal evils, such as sin and death. It is the wisdom which disillusions us about the fever for gold and power, and teaches us that goodness, love, charity, peace and greatness of soul are not acquired by means of money and wealth. It is dignified and industrious patience in the face of living with a scarcity of economic resources and in the midst of modest social conditions. It is conducive to praying, to working well, to hoping, to giving and loving, because it teaches confidence in Providence and a recognition of the worth of things and moral good. It is liberation of the spirit which, freed from the distractions of inferior goods, can act and love as spirit.

This is why we must face up to the consideration of Christian poverty in all seriousness, and never think of it as something anachronistic for us moderns, or absurd for those of us experts in sociological and economic matters.

And the more the increasing abundance of material goods tempts us to forget Christian poverty today, or hinders our practice of it, the more we must understand it and practice it properly. Without this interior virtue, we cannot work out our salvation; the words of Christ in this regard are impressively severe: "And Jesus said to his disciples, a rich man will not enter God's kingdom easily. And once again I tell you, it is easier for a camel to pass through a needle's eye, than for a man to enter the kingdom of heaven when he is rich" (Math. 19:23-24).

We must seek to find the reason for Christ's disturbing frankness regarding riches in the ease and the force with which riches disturb the mind of any man avid to possess them. Riches induce a man to think first that they are indispensable, then that they are supreme, and finally that they are the only thing that will answer all his needs, bestow complete security, satisfy all his desires, be the source of all power, and open the way to all the opportunities for happiness.

This is idolatry. This is a delusion which leads to bondage. Riches obtain their value from the service they render man. But if man does not treat them with a strong and free heart — that is to say, in the spirit of poverty — they will become his master and he their servant. They will rule his mind and heart, obscure any true vision of life and order, corrupt the affections of the soul and poison relationships among neighbors. They crush man under the weight of great anxiety. They smother all his aspirations towards nobler things, which are our true destiny. They debase moral life to the level of mediocrity and venal considerations. They inflate a man with vain pride, and empty the soul of all wise humility. They weaken the will and win it over easily to idleness, to boredom, to vice. They lead to hardness of heart and forgetfulness of the joy of giving without receiving.

In the end, riches can hinder loving, when Christianity is love; and impede prayer, when Christianity is communion with God.

These considerations, and others also which can be drawn from the Gospel concerning the danger of riches for the human soul, make us reflect on the gravity of this matter, and the necessity for finding an honest and satisfying solution. But the words of Jesus Christ sound so decisive and so solemn that we begin to doubt if we can find any such solution, just as the rich young man doubted

when he turned away from the Lord in sadness
after he had heard from his lips the words reserved
to those seeking perfection: "Go home and sell all
that belongs to thee, give it to the poor and so the
treasure thou hast shall be in heaven; then come
back and follow me!" (Math. 19:21-22). After
witnessing such an episode, the Apostles themselves doubted: "Who then can be saved?" It is a
grave question.

The Relationship between Religion and Economic Progress

The solution is to be found in the words of Jesus which give us the theme for our third observation: "such a thing is impossible to man's powers, but to God all things are possible" (Math. 19:26). This is an important affirmation. It teaches us that man cannot succeed in freeing himself from subjection to material goods by his own strength alone, but that he can rise above them with the help of God. They show us also that religion has an efficacious and salutary influence in restoring human liberty from the enchantment of earthly things.

Religion is thus indispensable in the life of man even in the domain of economics, if it be his will that temporal goods, at once invaluable and demanding, should not constitute a dead weight capable of drowning him in materialism with the consequent loss of the kingdom of God. Man must rather see them as only a gift of God, carrying responsibilities from which he can draw normal and real advantages for human life and for his eternal salvation. Only religion can give to economic reality a salutary equilibrium.

The separation that science and modern practices have effected between economics and morality, and thus between economics and religion, is one of the gravest errors of our time. Economics certainly has its special field of study, of method and of application, but it must not be wrenched from the higher and complete purpose of life, which only a moral and religious vision can give.

This fundamental observation suggests another clarifying consideration which we will borrow from St. Thomas. He teaches: "Created things by themselves do not separate us from God, but on the contrary they lead us to him. But if instead they should separate us from God, the fault lies with those who use them in an unreasonable manner." (S.Th.Iq.65, art.1ad3). What applies to created things in general must be applied in particular to riches. It is the use we make of them which determines them as good or bad; but since by nature they are useful, and tend to give personal and specific advantages primarily to the particular and immediate interest of the man who possesses them, they lend themselves to egoistic ends.

St. Ambrose himself, so severe in his denunciation of the dangers and the sins of the rich, explicitly affirms that the evil is not in the riches themselves but in the evil use we make of them.

From these basic truths is derived so much of the Church's teaching that we do not intend to expound them now. To get some idea of the doctrinal wealth of these affirmations, however, it will suffice to recall that the concept of economic goods, their origin, their purpose and their distribution engendered the famous social question which so preoccupies science, politics, and the economy — the very life of our society.

It is not for nothing that the Church, especially through the ministry and the teaching of the recent popes, has given such basic instructions on the social question, and thus indirectly on the whole ordering of material goods. We would do well to become familiar with this "social doctrine of the Church." In the crisis of social systems founded on the primacy of the economic order, be they capitalist or marxist, this doctrine is today a vindication and a defence for all those who are charged, not only with protecting the faithful by strengthening them in their adhesion to Christian social doctrine, but also with immunizing them against cringing sympathies for certain false theories. Furthermore, this social doctrine is also a vindication for all men of good will who are anxious to find in a system of authoritative, coherent and humane thought — namely, the thought of the Church —

a solid foundation upon which to rebuild our modern society.

The study of these problems obliges us to define certain concepts concerning material goods which are germane to our subject. For example, is the actual renunciation of temporal goods, that is, voluntary poverty, obligatory for profession of the Christian faith, or is it only a counsel of Christian perfection? What of the recommendation to give of our superfluity to the poor — or better still, what does the Gospel mean by "that which you have"? What is the standard for alms-giving and charity? "You should give alms out of the store you have" (Luke 11:41).

What about private property, and why must it be defended? Whence are derived its rights and its twofold function, private and social? Why should savings be encouraged? What is the relationship between justice and charity? And so on! The questions are numerous, and all of them seem to call for solutions based on the assumption we have been considering: that of an expanding economic well-being.

This very well-being has in many ways made it easier to find answers for some aspects of these questions. An instinctive dynamism seems to pervade the "economic mentality" of modern man, now that he is no longer bound up so tenaciously with his material possessions. He acquires them, changes them, and sells them with a much greater unconcern than in days gone by. Abundance has slaked in him the fearful hardness of avarice, and his faith in prosperity has made him more disposed to spending, to beneficence and to risks. The Christian mind can find certain points of harmony with this "economic mentality" where it tends to consider temporal goods as means and not as ends.

But we would prefer to leave the study of these problems to those who are interested, while we offer instead a few practical suggestions which we deem useful for Christian life in today's favorable economic climate.

PART TWO

The great precept which is valid in every field, and upon which Christianity is founded, is the precept of love: "It is all for you and you for Christ and Christ for God" (I Cor. 3:23).

Honesty, integrity, moderation in life — these are constant reminders of the end towards which economic means must lead us.

The Fundamental Attitude: Love

We are speaking here to those who can understand, to those who possess or who at least want to possess the "knowledge of Christ" (I Cor. 2:3).

Our first suggestion is much more than a counsel or a simple recommendation. It is a precept. Even more, it is the great precept upon which Christianity is based, the precept of love. It demands that we love God above all things and with all our strength, to a degree and intensity that is superlative. This is no empty phrase or vague sentiment. This is a command, a law from the mind of God which must find a living and forceful echo in all our hearts. This psychology of the love of God merits understanding and attention, especially today when the winds of greed blow harder and drive man from seeking his true purpose. St. Paul called this the "root of all evil" (I Tim. 6:10). All of us must learn anew to give to God, who is love, that place in our heart which belongs to him alone. All of us must reserve for this first and supreme act of our religion, the deepest, liveliest and fullest of sentiments.

Then there is the love of neighbour. This is another formidable precept which we must admit not having as yet practised to the fullness of its potentialities. Even if this be our intention, we are not achieving full effectiveness so long as the love of our neighbor has still not become so evident and real as to constitute the distinctive mark of our being Christians. "The mark by which all men will know you for my disciples will be the love you bear one another" (John 13:34).

We are a long way from practising the precept to the extent that we realize in our lives the double equation of the Gospel: we must love our neighbour as Christ has loved us, and we must love our neighbour as ourselves.

If in reality such a law did mold our lives, what an economy, what a sociology, what sort of a civil community would be the result? In this respect, Christianity appears still incomplete, and at the present moment almost at the beginning of a long new route.

Gratitude

Another religious duty flows from the greater economic well-being that our time bestows on us. It is gratitude towards Providence, which so disposes things as to invite our recognition and praise. We moderns are so tempted by short-sightedness that we do not know how to discover or even search for the paternal hand of God working behind the screen of our experience to give it a profound meaning. This is something which not all of us can understand, but which is always traceable to a source of infinite goodness. We do not see the hand of God giving our experience the value of a religious, spiritual and moral ascension.

This wise and religious view of the background against which life unfolds should be familiar especially to us Christians because it is drawn from an understanding of reality that is magnificently optimistic in the light of faith. It should prevail over the sombre and despairing vision that modern pessimism propagates so widely in philosophy, literature, and the theatre, the ghostly and anguished night into which the universe of the godless seems plunged.

It is not always easy for our limited faith to thank the Lord when we are in need and in pain. But it should be easier, and hence more imperative, when relative success, also in the material order, comforts us on our painful pilgrimage.

It would be well, then, if a prayer of thanksgiving to God became part of our piety: at table, at the end of the day, during happy moments as well as during moments of reflection and prayer. Such prayers, for example, as are offered at Mass on festive occasions.

The habit of gratitude towards God for his kindness to us teaches us also to be grateful towards our fellow men. Through affectionate ties of blood or friendship, or as a result of common membership in a civil organization, they are our helpers. We owe so much to the love and the work of others — and we forget so easily! We must take notice of the fact that a large part of social psychology, derived from the French Revolution and developed by the cultural, social and political movements which followed it, is impregnated with rancor, bitterness and hatred. Hence in the progress we make in living together as a society, we are still today intoxicated by a deadly atmosphere, and we find ourselves *a priori* critics and adversaries of civil organization itself, from which we indisputably derive benefits. This is a negative mentality belonging to the past and bereft of many of the historical reasons which gave it birth.

Modern economic and social conditions could allow us to surpass this morbid mentality and suggest a better, more serene, more positive and, if you wish, more democratic (understood as more flexible) human relationship due to our increasing well being, which is also more equitable and more fraternal. It is clear that the social spirit of Christianity, strong in its blend of justice and charity, inspires us and instills within us feelings of gratitude and respect for our society, better oriented to the welfare of all. It makes the informed Christian a grateful and friendly citizen.

The Three Negative Tendencies of Economic Well-being

It is necessary to pause a moment for another reflection, which tempers our theoretical optimism regarding economic well-being and warns of its inadequacy, whenever one seeks to raise it as the highest ideal of modern life or give it pre-eminent importance in our society. We cannot, in effect, eulogize economic well-being without pointing out anew certain reservations we had to make earlier in this regard.

Economic welfare tends to assume the first place in the scale of values. It seems to be the supreme good, the unique salvation, the end which justifies every effort and satisfies every aspiration. This tendency to overestimate economic well-being can assume a character that is anti-religious, or at least a-religious.

Secondly, the sovereign and exclusive pursuit of economic welfare reveals another tendency: self-centeredness. It tends to make absolute the person who is central either in the production or as the beneficiary of this production. Thus it can transform itself into something anti-social and make those who do not benefit from it the tools of whoever appears indispensable to secure it for them.

Thirdly, economic welfare can bring with it another negative tendency that is anti-moral when the ease that it procures renders life too comfortable, reduces effort, makes soul and body indolent, levels and standardizes everything, creates the mass man, devoid of originality or the ability to make his own decisions, who easily seeks sensual and immoral adventure to compensate for the insignificant life to which he feels himself reduced.

We speak of this in addition to some other practical recommendations for the good conduct of a Christian in a period of economic welfare.

Practical Directives for Christian Conduct

The first recommendation will be honesty. By honesty we understand here the uprightness of ancient times, justice which acknowledges and respects the rights of others in things which belong to them.

We must remember that the two commandments of God in this matter have lost none of their force: the seventh, do not steal; the tenth, do not covet the things of others.

Our society is moving towards a more equitable distribution of wealth. Modern economy is being organized on a more extended and more complicated scale in relation to the social community and we are on the way towards achieving a balance between economic development and social progress. Thus it is good to reaffirm the concept of private property by re-examining its forms of application and by recalling its two extremes:

1. Every man has the right to some things as property.

2. Every property must have a certain relationship to its public utility.

This is why all have the duty to respect the property of others and to contribute to the common good. No criticisms undermining private property, or any evolution in its concept or function, can remove its legitimate strength and its provident function not only as an institution of private property but also as a moral reality.

As Pius XII has well said: "Whoever wishes that the star of peace should rise and rule over society must give to work the place God assigned to it in the beginning. As an indispensable means to dominate the world as God has willed for his glory, all work possesses an inalienable dignity and at the same time is linked very closely with personal perfection ... These demands include ... the preserving and the perfecting of a social order which, no matter how modestly, affords an opportunity for private property on every level in society" (Christmas message, 1942).

It is certainly necessary that the limits of private property be defined by studying the basic human needs we call the "natural law," which is then further determined by positive laws.

It is permitted and even obligatory to promote social progress in accepted forms so as to effect equitable economic adjustments. But for this very reason, it is indispensable that the legal prescriptions which define and protect the property of economic goods, their production and their distribution, be rigorously observed.

A society in which economic legality is not respected is a decadent society, one which is wearing away the very fabric of its stability. Thus, the more one desires economic welfare, and the more it becomes widespread, the more vigorous and spontaneous must be the observance of the two commandments previously mentioned. Both private and public education must stress this observance. In the past, careless violations could perhaps find some excuse in the limited economic situation then prevailing, but today they merit an even stronger condemnation.

Honesty is a necessary rule of the social order. Whoever violates it sins not only against the man who is directly defrauded of what is his due, but against the community as a whole, for he shakes the social confidence which is the indispensable foundation of a civil community, and of its honor and its efficiency.

We must recommend to everyone, and especially to our faithful, the virtues proper to an economic situation such as ours, which is in the process of development and is so intimately linked to the social betterment of our people.

Here we shall simply offer a few indications from public opinion. We would like to have administrators of integrity, but reports of administrative disorders, venality in public officials, and shady dealings in the discharge of official duties are too frequent not to grieve us profoundly as citizens and as Catholics. In those who perform public duties, whether political, administrative, burcaucratic or disciplinary, we wish always to be able to honour an exemplary integrity. We would like the practice of our social life to be characterized always by disinterest and a faithful respect for the law. Commercial and fiscal fraud, contraband, mismanagement of public monies, bribery, theft, and especially the breaking of one's promises must be seen by everyone as evils which dishonor a society that was civilized by and founded upon Christian principles. These evils must be avoided and condemned by all.

There are other evils characteristic of an affluent society, such as manipulations on the stock exchange involving the detriment of others, gambling, excessive luxury. ... We are not competent to discuss these in detail but we are competent to deplore the damaging social and moral effects of such abuses of wealth. And we have the right to recall here especially the frightening words of Christ, "Woe upon you who are rich" (Luke 6: 24).

We have both the competence and the right to urge moderation in the use of the economic resources Providence places at our disposition. The end temporal goods are intended to serve must never be forgotten. They are to give man a decent life, not serve his pride, nor his vanity, nor his avarice, nor provide him with futile pleasures or vices. We must not forget the human values — of work, of suffering, of the needs of others — contained in money and goods, if we are to use them with moderation and even with reverence and gratitude.

Simplicity, thrift, and liberality in the use of material goods show the superiority of the soul over them and demonstrate its nobility and good taste.

Here we can recall how wise is that self-denial which the discipline of the Church urges upon us at given times and under special forms for moral and religious motives. Observance of these disciplinary norms and this spirit of austerity and penance both enables us to follow Christ faithfully and teaches us a better evaluation and use of the things of this world.

This appeal for simplicity and austerity of life, for detachment from money, from excessive comfort, and from any display of vanity we wish to direct particularly to our own clergy. We are bound in this matter more than others, by the tighter bonds which unite us to Christ and for the sake of the example others expect from us. We know the efficacy that the pursuit of poverty can give our ministry, and how sterile it becomes when it appears clothed in some vanity or inspired by mercenary considerations.

If we want to be authentic ministers of God, we must guard ourselves against all avarice, all commercial adventures, all worldliness. Even when seeking the material means necessary for good works and our ministry, we must never become insistent or indiscreet. The means must never appear more important than the ends towards which they are directed. Our search for the necessary material goods must always be transparently disinterested, a proof in itself of the poverty which inspired the search, and the charity which is the only end it is to serve.

In this connection there arises the vexing question of the offerings made for ceremonies that go with the performance of the sacred ministry. Let us recall the canonical prescriptions that no arbitrary charges may be made, that religious ceremonies may not be weighed down with burdensome and merely ornamental accretions. Devotions must never be permitted to assume a lucrative aspect or purpose. Keep all charges to a minimum, even legitimate stipends. Remember that the public is most sensitive on this score, and tends to criticize priests as well as their ministry in a biting and negative way.

Nothing, we believe, separates people from their religion today as much as the accusation, the suspicion, or the calumny of self-interest among ecclesiastics. Remember the words of the Apostle: "We are careful not to give offence to anybody, lest we should bring discredit to our ministry" (II Cor. 6:3).

This reminder does not concern merely the observance of disciplinary canons which require a certain exterior style of ecclesiastical life. It is rather an invitation to us all, priests and laymen, to discover an interior aspect of Christ's Church, which is precisely its poverty.

We wish to speak of the mystery of poverty within the great design of the Redemption. This design, we know, is a mystery of love which gives itself, makes a present of itself, and pours itself out so that in manifesting itself to the world it appears bereft and impoverished of all earthly goods, as if to demonstrate that no selfishness or worldly possessions should cover or qualify it.

Poverty will be the garment of Christ and of all

who are his whenever they wish to imitate, represent and proclaim him. The poor will be first in the kingdom of God, and the society born of Christ will not be founded on pomp, power, or trust in material goods, but rather on the emptiness of this world, on poverty, nourished by a wholly spiritual force, the help and sustenance from above. This is the economy of the Gospel which is perpetuated in the "Church of the Poor" (Ecclesia Pauperum, Phil. 2:6-7). This was said by the then reigning Pontiff, John XXIII, in proposing to the Ecumenical Council at the opening session this great subject for meditation and reform.

PART THREE

The poor man is the mirror of Christ, indeed almost a living sacrament of Him.

The work of mercy is not born of fear, or compulsion, or self-interest; it does not seek recognition or sympathy, praise or gratitude, but it is born of love for God and for the brethren.

"Blessed are the merciful; they shall obtain mercy." Math. 5:7.

Love and Help the Poor

We must have for the poor man a special reverence and a great concern. He is the mirror of
Christ, as it were a living sacrament of him. He is
both a stimulus and the object of acts of charity.
He is our brother and his needs, even if they are
not rights in themselves, put us under obligation
to him. If we pass him by, he makes us uneasy, but
if we help him he brings us joy. He teaches us to
live well, if we will hear his silent lesson. He is a
travelling companion who, if we look closely, is always with us. As Jesus said: "You have the poor
among you always" (Math. 26:11).

This evangelical prophecy still holds true among
us, even at this period of affluence. Consider our
modern world, which seems finally to have at-
tained a degree of efficiency sufficient to allow it
to obtain its daily bread. Is that enough? No, it is
still not enough. It is not enough here in our own
country, where a great number of people still do
not have enough bread to sustain a normal life and
a natural development. We must not be deceived
by this growing prosperity. It is still not evenly
distributed, nor is it yet sufficiently secure. It is

not yet equal to the task of providing for a great many needs. This is why we must, at the same time that we are analyzing the meaning of affluence, still encourage those forces which produce it and guarantee it.

As economic prosperity places greater resources at our disposal, we must think immediately of alms-giving. This is an old but a hallowed word.

The Bible speaks of the duty of alms-giving, its piety, its virtue — redeeming for the giver, consoling for the recipient. The whole of Christian tradition shines forth in these acts of individual goodness and social providence. Alms-giving is a part of ascetics, of pedagogy, and of social Christianity. It is so much a part of the spirit of the Gospels that it is described by some of the Gospels' most essential and most authentic expressions: providence, mercy, charity.

Today we call it charity, aid, help, relief, or some other name, but the concept should remain what it originally was, namely, the spontaneous gift of an economic value to an indigent brother, not so that he remain indigent, but rather that he may rise above his need and become able to take care of himself. The offering must be made freely, out of love — and let us say it once and for all, out of love for God. The work of mercy is perfect when it takes its beginning and its value from the heart of him who gives, not from fear or compulsion or from some hidden self-interest, or from a desire to receive in the giving some merit or special regard from the recipient, or praise or gratitude from any quarter. It is enough that God has seen the good heart within and the hidden gesture without.

If we are looking for a genuine and purifying expression of our Christian life, we should cultivate again the practice of this salutary charity.

Our thoughts go out to our charitable works — especially to the activities of the societies of St. Vincent de Paul, who have made this charitable effort a defence and a school of living faith, as well as a source of humble and very human consolation. Our thoughts go out to thousands of others; yes, thousands, because, thanks to God, innumerable are the charitable institutions, forms and activities that still flourish in the Catholic world. We would like all of them, in this time of economic affluence, to become more fruitful and helpful, better organized and more efficient, increasingly active and efficacious, and always inspired by the spirit of Christ, always free and detached, always prompt and friendly, always generous and silent.

Invitation to Charity and Sacrifice

May all Christians, but especially the young, heed the urgency of the unmistakable teaching of the Gospel. For it is the young who are most tempted to make themselves a law unto themselves, and squander their money without thinking of the toil and drudgery it took to earn it, or the use for which it was destined. Yet they are also the most sensitive to the obligation to help those who suffer, even at the cost of personal sacrifice. They do not want to avoid a personal participation in the humble, concrete, always modern forms of personal charity. They are aware of the moral energy and civic effectiveness which spring from the positive exercise of human and Christian compassion. The desire for social reform, no matter how noble and perceptive, cannot guarantee its own sincerity unless it is supported by a direct and lively awareness of the needs of others.

We all have another duty, related to the primary obligation of Christian charity, and that is to impose some sacrifices on ourselves and to save what we can, so as to have something of our own to offer to persons and to worthy institutions which lack the necessary means to support themselves. This duty opens up large "catholic" horizons, that is to say, horizons that are ecumenical and universal. For today we have all become citizens of the world, and our neighbour may be someone far from us geographically.

This sense of universality should be highly developed in a Christian and Catholic community such as our own. It should manifest itself concretely in a hand extended or a purse opened to our unknown brothers far away who are moving towards a modern civilization. Milan has a tradition of generosity in this respect that stretches far into its past and which must be revitalized today. The example of the German Catholics in their collective gesture of penitential saving and ecumenical charity is worthy of admiration and imitation.

So that charity may benefit from economic means by allowing them to serve great spiritual ends, and because of the immense need now existing, we speak of "days," which means collections. These we must promote and recommend to the generosity of good people: a Seminary Day, a Day for Building New Churches, Mission Day, a Day for a Catholic University, for the Catholic Press, for Catholic Action, for still other things, be they national, diocesan or local. What is the meaning of these "days"? They show that there still exist enormous and evident needs which have no other sources of help than spontaneous and benevolent charity. They show our poverty, the honor of the Church today, which forces us to suffer and to beg for works and plans that our ministry cannot abandon.

It is well that we understand this fact: the Church always lacks resources proportionate to its mission. The Church is forbidden secular activity for economic gain. In this hour when others are affluent, the Church is passing through a critical period of growing needs with absolutely insufficient resources with which to meet them. It is here that our hope quickens, not only for our own profit and comfort but for the benefit of all good works, that the hour of economic affluence may become the hour of charity. In this way it may also become the hour of justice and peace.

Economic Welfare as an Instrument of Evangelical Charity

The desire to transform temporal riches into evangelical charity is so characteristic of good Catholics that the already numerous "days" for collecting the necessary material means, that I mentioned above, were found to be so insufficient that the faithful have initiated new and other worthy projects. These merit our mention and our warm approval.

Some will say that the demands are too numerous. We do not wish to be indiscreet nor to appear to speak out of self-interest, but we believe we do not err in observing that the streams of money spent on entertainment and luxuries are still very considerable, and not very edifying when compared to offerings for charity. We must temper with Christian charity the excess we invest in pagan hedonism, human selfishness and creature comfort. There are also some enormous fortunes which could well make amends for the questionable or at best overly facile way in which they were made. There are immense and stagnant riches still to become responsible and worthy by adopting a charitable and social dimension. Meantime, they weigh heavily on those who guard them so jealously, often without knowing how to enjoy them wisely.

This is why we dare again to repeat the words of our Lord: "Blessed are the merciful; they shall obtain mercy" (Math. 5:7); "the measure you award to others is the measure that will be awarded to you" (Luke 6:38). We dare to hope that the development of the economy of material goods, which today consumes so much of human interest, will not become a detriment to the society which produces and enjoys them, but rather will be to its moral and temporal advantage.

Make it your first care to find the kingdom of God, and his approval, and all these things shall be yours without the asking. Math. 6:33.

Conclusion

Having examined some aspects of the nature, the dangers and functions of material goods, it seems necessary also to encourage and to bless the effort with which they are produced, the wisdom which regulates their distribution and use, and the charity which ennobles them. We close with the words Pope John XXIII used to end his encyclical *Mater et Magistra*, that whenever room is made for an awareness of spiritual values and supernatural ends in temporal affairs and institutions, these are invigorated by an efficacious regard for their specific and immediate purposes. The words of our Divine Master are still true: "Make it your first care to find the kingdom of God, and his approval, and all these things shall be yours without asking" shall be yours without asking" (Math. 6:33).

Printed in Canada by
HARPELL'S PRESS CO-OPERATIVE,
Gardenvale, Que.